When Dead Birds
See the Light

Quynh Nguyen

GLASSSPIDERPUBLISHING

This is a love letter to love, to everyone who has helped me in the creation of this book, and to A.

Contents

DAWN

I set myself on fire
Ablaze with hope
Love is the armor
You, the cause

Empty handed
No weapon
Armor lost
Dented
Fallen in the ash of hope

In the aftermath of war
I hear echoes of weekends past
Ghosts of days and nights
Warm memories that smell of summer rain

Dry, wet, fire, earth, rain
Mossy green, like my heart
Afresh with hope
Glistening in the morning dew.

ENTWINED

You make me feel safe
When we're entwined

The chaos out there
Is still out there
Running amok
Spreading wildfires
A sky of red
But it'll take a break
When we're entwined

We're on an oasis
We're in a green space
We're taking our vaccination
We're building a fortress

Not one welded from steel, not one made of
drugs, not one built on land
Not one that will constrict, weaken or
crumble

But one that is fluid, expansive, overflowing
and infinite

A world of leisure
When we're entwined.

ANARCHY

Love
You told me
What you have for me is love

Can I ask you
About love itself?
For the chaos it brings
For the beauty it creates
For the troubles it promises
And the atonement it gives

Love
You told me
What you have for me is a kind of craziness
That lives in the name of love

Love
You told me
It makes sense
To love me
It is the only meaning
It is the only way

Wedging a knife through chaos
Making sense through anarchy

Love
Or is it the anarchy of love?
A hope to rise up
A desire to bring down
A longing to shatter
Corpses shackled to our feet
Shadows shackled to our hearts

Is it the anarchy of love
Morphing hearts and burning souls?
Is it the anarchy of love
Like a knife cutting through butter?
Is it the anarchy of love
Blinding daylight, cutting through the night?
Is it the anarchy of love
The first of sound cutting through silence?
Is it the anarchy of love
Forging chaos out of order?
Is it the anarchy of love?
Is it just anarchy?

Just anarchy
A finger to the establishment
A cry out to the status quo
A silent weeping for all of us
Corpses flowing like water.

ETERNITY

I asked to stretch a moment into eternity
A moment I can walk into
Touch
Smell
Hear
And savor

I hoped to stretch a moment
Into reality
Into you
Into us

A moment in eternity
Or eternity in a moment
A thousand years or a thousand universes
Converge into this one space of ours
A moment in eternity
Or eternity in a moment

A thousand words and a thousand kisses
Converge
In space
Stretch
In time
Live
In reality

If I asked to stretch a moment into eternity
Would you want it to last, would you stay?
All I need is a little bit more time
To watch us unfold
To watch us just be
us

What do I need to
give in order to
get a moment of
eternity
by your side?

ACHE

If I could see into the future
Could I ask to see us?
I'd see you in your most common rituals
Crossing the street, drinking coffee, talking to
your lover
Someone I don't know and will never

If I could see into the future
I would write me out as
The background, the prequel, the past
The unfathomable space of what has been

If I could see into the future
I wouldn't see us
I would meet strangers whose lives I have
yet
Come to know

That's why the future is a place that doesn't
exist
For even if the world
Would become a better place

And you and I
Better people
The we that we have yet to create
Would not be there when the world becomes
a better place.

GHOSTS

They say
I live in the past
Listen to dead people
And converse with memories

But what if I tell you
It made better sense
When things first started

Before a war became a fight for greed
Before ideals became vessels for power
Before people got crushed to build cities
Before gods were turned into money
And before love was made bite-sized
and thumb-friendly
Before we were all slaves
To our own thirst and lust and hunger
Before blindness became our eyes

You say
I live in the past
Making friends with relics

Climbing into bed with nostalgia
But don't you see nostalgia is all I've got
When your words are cutting through me
Your presence is tainting my memories
Of you

Why can't you see
It made better sense
When things first got started?
When we were true.
When we were true.

PLANET

Sometimes I think I am from a different
Planet, a far, faraway
One that doesn't have you
And what I so dearly call life

One with a different home
A different kind of
Life and death
A different set of
Family and friends

One that sometimes I see through the
Hole of my dreams, the
Windows of my subconscious, the
Iceberg underneath the tip, the
Vastness of longing, the
Enormity of desire, the
Endless darkness, the
Eternal tunnel

Sometimes I feel a calling to return to
My Home, a place I can't visit
My Origin, a place I don't know
My Beginning, a place I can't see
My Ending, a place I can't reach

Sometimes on this Planet I am scorched
Not by our burning Sun
But by the invisibility of our existence
Falling onto our shoulders
It is too heavy
And I wish to return
To a Planet where it could be light

A far, faraway land
Would you be there?
Would you come?
Would you lead the way
Or follow the darkness?
Would you take a leap?
Would you make a pledge

And forget your eyes?
Leave behind your world
Your possessions
Your belongings
Your desires
And just walk toward love?

TO MY GRANDMA (i)

I heard a silent prayer
in the eyes you looked at me
words failed to mean
as your world no longer serves you

people you know are now dead
ghosts of yesterdays
people of your past
your children, crying in your dreams
those unborn unable to speak
unable to have form
unable to grasp at life

it was the war
the burning fires
the raging bombs
saigon was under siege
you hid your pain
underneath the
loose tunics that could no longer
hide the lost souls long dead
before they were born

who could dare to compare
the pain of a mother losing
her sons and daughters
to the pain of a country
losing
to another country.

TO MY GRANDMA (ii)

Last night I dreamt of you
You came into my dream
In the form of a bird
You were dancing
And you knew my name.

Last night I dreamt of you
You with your beautiful long hair and your
ageless face
You as beautiful as ever
Like the young girl you always were,
Untainted by the scars of time
You were smiling
And you knew my name.

Last night I dreamt of you
In a beautiful garden
Of numerous flowers and an endless sea of
grass

You were everywhere
You were the air
And you knew my name.

Why would I ever think
that I had lost you for good
When in fact you are just merely:
Awakened
At one with the world
And always
By my side.

DEAD BIRD

Ding dong
Woke up in the middle of the night
Someone I love is no longer here
The desert is getting bigger
Dryer
Colder

The bird is lying there
Cold and flayed
Trying in vain
Flapping its flapless wings
The memory of our love
Is buried in shame

Ding dong
Squinted!
The ray of sun has come
Dappled, blotched, tainted
The desert is coming into light
Its carcasses
Blown to pieces

Sudden quiver!
The wind has come
The carcass of our love lying there
Beaten black and blue
I'm scavenging
I'm bringing us home.

WARRIORS

We look at each other with those eyes
that aim to silence more than invite
When was the time
when words sang vocals of our love?
Now they just convey meaningless
courtesies
endless accusations
to no end

We are warriors
Skilled
Weapons ready at hand
Welded, sharpened, ready to leap
to hurt
to wound

No armors, the flesh bleeds
the heart enfeebled, muted
by the gaze
A dead gaze

Lover's tiffs
Meaningless fights
What are we doing
hurting
while we still love so much?

Day after,
the morning light comes
It cleanses
my sins, my pains, my confabulations

We look at each other with those eyes
head-first diving into the deep end of
a wordless forgiveness,
a hushed realization,
a hungry kind of
love that might
drown
lovers who are not
warriors like we are.

SEEING

I run out of ink
To describe you, my love
The endless beauty of your face
Instantly lit up
By the delight in your smile

I run out of time
To know how much love is enough
For you to feel full
Feel needed
Feel warm
In the embrace of my love

I run out of tricks
To surprise you
With every twist and turn of fate
To evade and elude
The warmth of your heart
Pulls me back in

I run out of excuses
My love
They were my refuge my facade my cave
I am in front of you love
As you and I and knowing we are more than
you and I

I run out of lines, my love
In front of you, I am silent
For a thousand words are being said
A thousand stars are getting aligned
A thousand birds are singing
A thousand miles only bring us here to this
moment

I run out of lies
For the truth is always ever ready to be said
And no lies can ever shield a truth
Shining brightly as you are

I run out of space, my love
The world is too small, for it to contain us

Everywhere I look, it's your presence
Everywhere I go, it's your space
And when I go back to mine
You are already there.

HOLY

I wanted to remember
But I can't
The last time my heart was intact

It was before we met

My heart knew no pain
No joy
No love
It was vain, selfish, bored
Strutting through the night like a diva queen
Proud and hollow
Crying on her pillowcase at night

I wanted to remember
But I can't
The last time I felt no fear

Now fear grips at my heart like smoke
Unable to clear, I try
To gasp for
Air that's the essence of you

I wanted to remember
But I can't
The last time my path had no point of gravity

Now I walk toward you
My steps light, hopeful,
As if love could materialize into a
Spring
In my steps

My love,
My love for you
Expands
With every second past

My heart
Trembles
With every thought of you

And I
Kneel down
In the presence
Of love.

WORDLESS

Darling
my love
my light
you never need words
when you talk to me

Darling
my sun
my friend
our souls meet before our tongues do

Let's not waste time
forming words
putting together grammar
errors are made with the greatest intention
lies are told in perfect form
and half-truths are masked as deep wisdom

Darling
please do not hesitate
let us
take a leap

run
dive headfirst
swim
go boldly into the night
touch
see with our hearts
now bare naked
trembling
shivering
with joy.

SPRING

Where did you go
My lover
Come back
Fill this mouth with
Lush green
Warm sunlight
And every drop of dew
I'll lap it up

Desert in my mouth
It has gone dryer and dryer
With every second past
With you gone, I'm basking in
The shadow of love
Adding lustre
To every single frame of you

Come back to our fresh meadows
To our bed of grass and greens that has just
been born

Everything glowing up, softening up in the
presence of love
Melting into a personal day

Come back to our sea of lush green
Drops of rain on the body of this earth fusing
with
Beads of sweats on our own bodies
Submit under this pleasurable pressure
Submerge like waves
Surrendering into the immense ocean

Come back to our bed of sun
A kind of warmth spreading slowly
But surely
Into the depths of our hearts
Filling up the crevices of our whole beings

Come back and together we will
Water this desert
And together we will
Let life spring.

HYMN

Let my love not become your poison
Let it not cloud your mind
Or confuse your judgment

Let my love not become your worry
Making you grow distant and cold
Or dampening your heart

Let my love not trap you inside its
Wants and needs
Expectations and high hopes
Moats and gates

Let my love not become a maze
Tricking and ensnaring you
Like a helpless prey
Shot by a skillful hunter

Let my love not become your darkness
Your vice
Your go-to only when you have got no other
choice

Let my love be your kingdom
Your light
Your song of joy
Let my love fill your space
Let it take you away on multiple escapes
Into whirlwinds of romance or depths of
hope
Across all loops of time
Let it wake in you the spirit
To love to fight to live
Let it take your soul and my soul
And join them in a warmest embrace.

About the Author

Quynh Nguyen is a young poet who lives and works in Saigon, Vietnam. A bilingual thinker and writer in Vietnamese and English, she traverses both worlds with a deep sense of curiosity and wonder. *When Dead Birds See the Light* is her first collection of poetry.

About the Publisher

Glass Spider Publishing was founded in 2016 by writer Vince Font to help independent and self-published authors reach readers through professionally edited and artfully designed books. The company is headquartered in Ogden, Utah, but has published authors throughout the world including the United States, Canada, England, Kenya, South Korea, and (as of this publication) Vietnam.

GLASS
SPIDER
PUBLISHING

www.glassspiderpublishing.com